The FURRY Alphabet Book

by Jerry Pallotta
Illustrated by Edgar Stewart

Charlesbridge

To Joe Doherty, my best English teacher.

To Annie, for her love and support, and her enduring patience.

Published by
Charlesbridge Publishing
85 Main Street
Watertown, MA 02172
(617) 926-0329

Library of Congress Cataloging-in-Publication Data
Pallotta, Jerry.
   The furry alphabet book / by Jerry Pallotta; illustrated by Edgar Stewart.
      p.   cm.
   Summary: Readers use the alphabet to learn about some of the more unusual mammals of the world.
   ISBN 0-88106-682-6 (library reinforced)
   ISBN 0-88106-465-3 (trade hardcover)
   ISBN 0-88106-464-5 (softcover)
   1. Mammals–Juvenile literature.   2. English language–Alphabet–Juvenile literature.
[1. Mammals.   2. Alphabet.]   I. Stewart, Edgar, 1959 - ill.   II. Title.
QL706.2.P35   1991
599— dc20   90-80287
[E]   CIP
                                                             AC

Printed in Italy by STIGE Turin
(sc)   10   9   8   7   6
(hc)   10   9   8   7   6   5   4   3   2

Books by Jerry Pallotta
   The Icky Bug Alphabet Book
   The Icky Bug Counting Book
   The Bird Alphabet Book
   The Ocean Alphabet Book
   The Flower Alphabet Book
   The Yucky Reptile Alphabet Book
   The Frog Alphabet Book
   The Furry Alphabet Book
   The Dinosaur Alphabet Book
   The Underwater Alphabet Book
   The Victory Garden Vegetable Alphabet Book
   The Extinct Alphabet Book
   The Desert Alphabet Book
   The Spice Alphabet Book
   The Make Your Own Alphabet Book
   Going Lobstering
   Cuenta los insectos (The Icky Bug Counting Book)

Special thanks to St. Nick and his reindeer.

A is the first letter of Aye-Aye.
This spooky-faced animal is
very hard to find. Not many
people have ever seen one
alive. It lives in the thick
forests of Madagascar, Africa.
The Aye-Aye uses its
teeth and its long
middle finger to dig in trees
for insects
to eat.

A a

B b

B is for Beaver. A Beaver has webbed feet and is an excellent swimmer. It uses its flat tail as a rudder to make sharp turns in the water. Did you know that a Beaver has to gnaw on trees to wear its front teeth down? A Beaver's front teeth never stop growing longer.

C is for Cheetah. It is the fastest animal on land. It is almost the fastest animal in the world, but a few birds can fly faster than a Cheetah can run. It looks like a blur when it runs past you.

Cc

The Cheetah can run fast for only a short distance. Then it has to stop and catch its breath. Of all the big cats, the Cheetah is one of the easiest to recognize because the spots on its fur look like black polka-dots.

D d

D is for Dingo. The Dingo is a wild dog from Australia. From far away Dingoes look tame and friendly just like other dogs. However, Dingoes are fierce.

E is for Ermine. The Ermine is a weasel. When winter comes, the color of its fur changes from brown to pure white. The white fur allows it to hide in the ice and snow.

E e

Ff

F is for Flying Squirrel. Flying Squirrels cannot really fly. Flying Squirrels do not have wings, but they do have furry flaps of skin between their front and back legs that they spread out like a kite. They climb trees and then glide from one tree to another tree. People have seen them glide for distances longer than a football field.

G is for Golden Lion Marmoset.
Golden Lion Marmosets are
New World monkeys. When they
have babies, they always have
twins. The fuzz around their faces
makes them look like lions.

Hey, nice fuzzy face!

G g

H is for Hyrax. Scientists tell us that the Hyrax is the animal most closely related to the elephant. At first glance — even at second glance — it does not seem possible that they could be related. The Hyrax is so small and the elephant is so big!

Hh

I i

I is for Ibex. Oh no! Not another animal that ends with the letter X. Male Ibexes smash their heads into each other to see who is tougher. Ibexes have great balance. They can headbutt each other while standing on steep rugged ground.

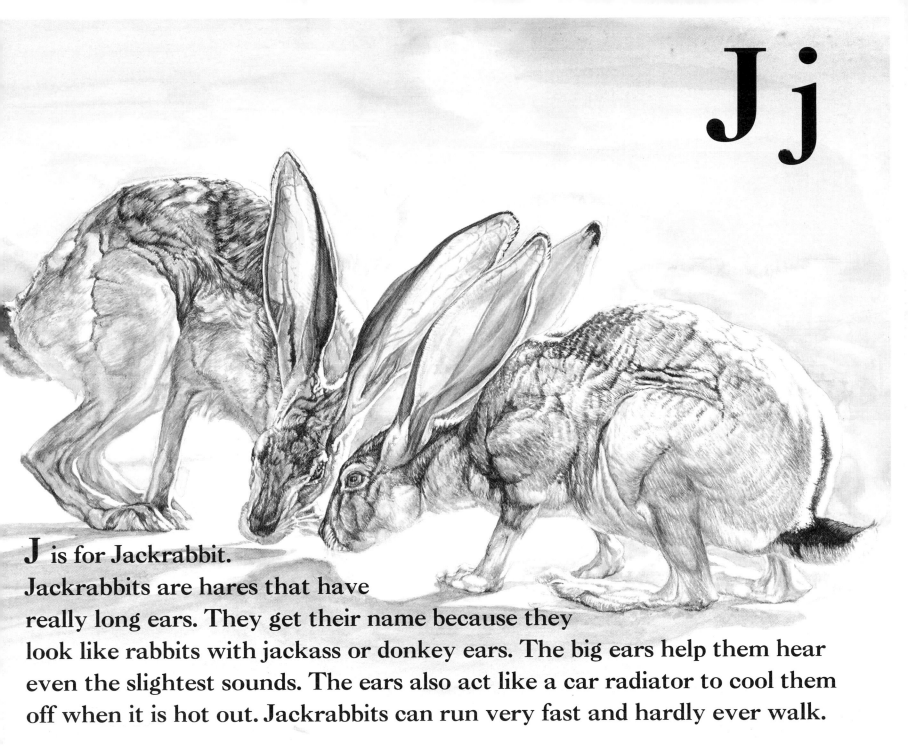

J j

J is for Jackrabbit.
Jackrabbits are hares that have
really long ears. They get their name because they
look like rabbits with jackass or donkey ears. The big ears help them hear
even the slightest sounds. The ears also act like a car radiator to cool them
off when it is hot out. Jackrabbits can run very fast and hardly ever walk.

K k

K is for Kangaroo Rat. These small rodents are called Kangaroo Rats because of their big hind legs. When they hop around, they use their tails for balance, just like kangaroos. Kangaroo Rats are found in the United States and should not be confused with the smallest kangaroo, the rat-kangaroo.

L is the first two letters of Llama. The vicuna, the guanaco, and the Llama are all similar. All three are related to the camel, but they have no humps on their backs. When Llamas get upset, they kick, hiss, and refuse to move. Sometimes they will even spit.

Ll

M is for Musk Ox. Years ago, the people of China gave the United States two panda bears. In return, the President of the United States gave the Chinese two Musk Oxen. Adult Musk Oxen protect their young by forming a circle around them.

M m

N is for Numbat. Numbats are also called Banded Anteaters. They use their pointed noses to poke around for termites, their favorite food. Numbats have more teeth than any other land animal, but they swallow their meals whole.

N n

O o

O is for Okapi. This shy animal
is similar to a giraffe, but it does
not have a really long neck and really long legs.
Okapis hide in the thick jungles of Central Africa.

P is for Proboscis Monkey. Wow! What a nose! The male
Proboscis Monkey has such a large nose that he uses one
of his hands to move his nose out of the way while he feeds
himself with his
other hand.

P p

Q q

Q is for Quokka. There are more than sixty types of kangaroos and all of them come from Australia and the surrounding islands. The Quokka is one of the smaller kangaroos. All kangaroos are marsupials. A marsupial is a mammal that carries its babies in a pouch.

Hey, who is that guy with the furry face and what is he doing in this book?

Oh! That's right! People are mammals too!

Rr

R is for Reindeer. Reindeer are also called Caribou. They migrate in huge herds from one area to another, looking for food to eat. Reindeer have large hooves that prevent them from sinking into the snow. A doe is a deer, a female deer. A Reindeer doe is the only female deer that has antlers.

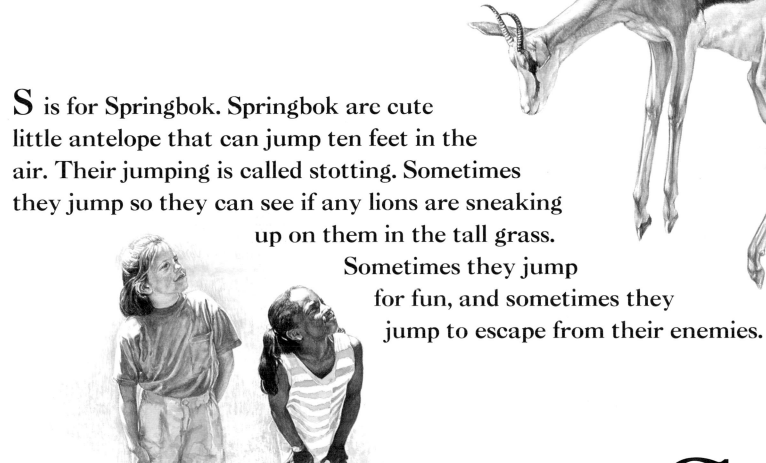

S is for Springbok. Springbok are cute
little antelope that can jump ten feet in the
air. Their jumping is called stotting. Sometimes
they jump so they can see if any lions are sneaking
up on them in the tall grass.
Sometimes they jump
for fun, and sometimes they
jump to escape from their enemies.

S s

T is for Tarsier. A Tarsier's eyes are so huge that they are bigger than its brain. It can turn its head almost completely around, which helps it hunt at night. A Tarsier catches and eats live bugs, spiders, and sometimes lizards.

T t

U is for Unau.
The Unau is a
Two-toed Sloth.
Sloths are one of
the slowest animals
in the world. They
are so slow and so
inactive that green
mold often grows on
their fur. The Unau and the
three-toed sloth both like to hang
upside-down from trees.

Uu

V is for Vizcacha. This rodent is considered a nuisance. It burrows and makes tunnels in the ground. Sometimes the tunnels cave in, and horses and other animals fall into the holes and break their legs. Do you think the Vizcacha looks like a combination of a squirrel, a mouse, and a rabbit?

V v

W is for Wallaroo. Wallaroo, how are you? Wallaroos are big kangaroos, but not the biggest. A group of kangaroos is called a mob. The leader is the "old man." The males are called "boomers," the females are called "does," and the babies are called "joeys." Where's joey?

W w

X is for Xukazi. In southern Africa, the Xhosa people speak the Zulu language. They call a female lamb a Xukazi. There are not many wild land mammals that start with the letter X.

Instead of "Mary had a little lamb," maybe they sing, "Mary had a little Xukazi."

X x

Yy

Y is for Yapok. The Yapok is the only marsupial that lives in and around water. It is an aquatic marsupial. Some people call it a Water Opossum. When the mother Yapok swims, she can close her pouch so that her babies will not get wet.

Z z

Z is for Zorilla. This animal is a zillion times smellier than the smelliest skunk. Whew!

It was once reported that several lions were about to eat a zebra that they had just killed when, all of a sudden, a Zorilla showed up. The smell was so bad that the lions stayed away until the Zorilla was long gone.

What's going on here?
Hey, stop eating the book!

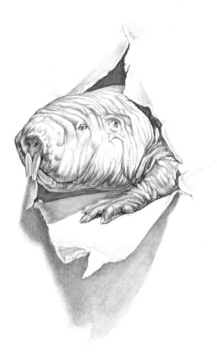

Sorry, Naked Mole Rat. You are a mammal, but you do not have any fur, and you are also quite ugly. You should not be in this book,
not even at

The End.

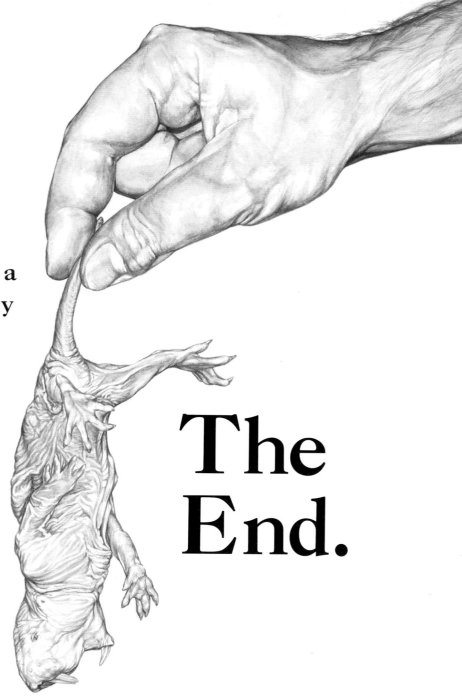